START TO DRAW

Axelle Vanquaillie

START TO

Visual Communication
in the Workplace

LANNOO
CAMPUS

TABLE OF CONTENTS

YOU REALLY SHOULD READ THIS BOOK IF YOU...

◯ Manage people and want to involve them in a story

◯ Are a student who wants to have notes for which others are prepared to pay

◯ Want to give presentations that everyone will remember

◯ Want to take your communication to the next level

◯ Teach and want to inspire students

◯ Want to show that you really listen as a counsellor and mediator

◯ Are a trainer or coach and want to stand out from the all the rest by giving tangible insights

◯ Can reflect better when you are drawing

◯ Think better while drawing or scribbling

◯ Like to draw

◯ Are looking for a creative outlet

Tick who you are!

Are you one of the 5 out of 100 people who are not visual at all? If so, don't buy this book for yourself. Buy it for someone else and make them happy!

INTRODUCTION

Once upon a time, a teenager attended a strict catholic school for girls. One warm afternoon, as her thoughts were straying off, her music teacher told her about *Peter and the Wolf*, a musical fairy tale by Sergei Prokofiev written for the Moscow Youth Theatre in 1936 – a simple and compelling story, easy to understand, and intended primarily for children. The piece became a worldwide sensation and beguiled young and old.

Her textbook was on her desk. Dozens of pages that proved that the teacher's monotonous explanation was the truth. The words and letters were dancing before her eyes.

The girl began to draw. She chose a random blank page from her book. Peter was the first to appear on the sheet, followed by the forest where Peter heads against his grandfather's advice. And finally, all the characters of the story, such as the wolf, the duck, the bird, and the instruments for which the story was written: the oboe, the clarinet, the flute... The girl was fully absorbed in the story, as if in a dream.

Then the dream was suddenly interrupted. The teacher had appeared unexpectedly in front of the girl's desk. "What on earth are you doing?" she asked. "Shouldn't you be paying attention? You draw in art class, not during music lessons!"

The girl was confused... She had never been more attentive to her lessons.

Twenty-five years later, now an experienced organisational coach, the girl became acquainted with visual facilitation and visual reporting. She discovered that drawing is just as impactful in professional business life as *Peter and the Wolf*: simple, easy to understand and compelling for young and old. From that day on, she decided that she would never, ever give up drawing.

HOW THIS BOOK CAME TO LIFE

As soon as I got my first taste of visual work, I felt driven to share my experiences and tips. Every time I experienced the impact of drawing, I thought "everyone should know how to do this."

So it became my mission to inspire at least 1000 people a year to start drawing... Not as a form of art, but as a way to communicate effectively. I have been in far too many presentations, workshops and meetings that lacked impact. I strongly believe that by using drawing, you can convey your message a lot more clearly and engagingly.

I started training courses and workshops so that people could see for themselves just how quickly you can develop the skill. But I felt that it was not enough. Many of my students asked for a workbook that would bring all my tips and tricks together. And so the idea for this book started to grow. It would be in an easy-to-read format, teeming with tips. I planned to explain the basic principles of drawing, and to answer the most frequently asked questions. Easier said than done, it seemed.

The turning point was the day my friend Caroline helped me to define the scope and content of the book. She had attended several of my courses and workshops and summarised the key insights and the most frequently asked questions. She kept pulling at my sleeve and helped me with the writing. Thanks to that, and her fresh view, I eventually managed to produce the book.

I hope you will enjoy reading it, but above all that you will have a lot of fun drawing.

WHY DRAWING WORKS...

We all are visual creatures.

Did you know?
1. The retina of the eye is an outgrowth of the brain. Half of our brain is devoted to processing visual information.
2. Neurons for this function take up about 30% of the cortex, while only 8% are for touch and 3% for hearing.
3. If we catch sight of an image even for as brief a time as 13 milliseconds, our brain can still identify it.*
4. At least 65% of us are visual learners. Dr Richard Felder's research established this in the 1980s, laying the foundation for understanding that we have different learning styles. Further studies have shown that even more of us are visual learners than Dr Felder found – maybe up to 8 out of every 10 people.
5. We have a remarkable ability to remember pictures. We can remember 2000 pictures with at least 90% accuracy.
6. Presentations with visuals are 43% more persuasive than textual ones.
7. Seeing is believing. What our eyes see can influence what we hear. Watching someone's lips move can trick the brain into hearing the wrong sound. This is called the McGurk effect, after the scientist who made the discovery.

This explains exactly why a picture is worth a thousand words.

*(T. Romih, PhD in Nanotoxicology, Seyens.com, 2016)

Drawing sparks communication and enhances:
- memorisation
- ordering and simplifying complex information
- understanding
- talking and listening

And above all...
it is a universal language! You don't need to speak the same language to understand a picture.

Did you know?

Drawing is one of the oldest forms of human expression. Evidence of its existence precedes that of written communication, with rock paintings dating to around 30,000 years ago. These drawings, known as pictograms, depicted objects and abstract concepts.

A SNAPSHOT OF MODERN LIFE

We live in a rapidly changing world.
Huge amounts of information and data are at our fingertips, and we expect it to be presented clearly and concisely, "here and now".
We rarely read articles to the end.
In a matter of minutes, we watch and swap videos.
Over recent years, our attention span has decreased to only 8 seconds, which is less than that of a goldfish.
We find it more and more difficult to focus on one thing for very long.

It's clear that getting and keeping the attention of your audience is a huge challenge. The use of pictures, in this case drawings, reinforced by storytelling, works with that 8-second attention span. And it's not something I invented. There's even a name for it: the picture superiority effect. You have probably noticed that if you post pictures on social media, you get more likes than if you use text.

It's clear that we live in a visual culture. Yet most of us haven't found – let alone mastered – an easy way to translate our thoughts into drawings.

This fascinates me. Although we all enjoyed drawing as children, we dropped it from our communication skill set when we grew up.

How did you start out with this?

In 2010, I took part in a congress on conflict media-
tion. At that congress, I saw a graphic recorder for
the first time. She listened to the speakers and
summarised everything live on a large piece of
paper. And I said to myself, if that is a job, then you
must be the happiest person in the world... and I
even felt a little jealous. A few months later, I heard
that she was organising a two-day training course
on the subject, so I signed up. And in the wake of
the training, I was fully occupied and started to draw
everywhere that was suitable... or sometimes where
it was perhaps less suitable.

DRAWING AT WORK

The modern approach of using visuals to support business change processes, transformation and strategy started in the sixties and seventies in the San Francisco Bay Area. With the aim of working more effectively, pioneers like Michael Doyle, David Straus, David Sibbet, Geoff Ball and Doug Engelbart, and MG Taylor – all in diverse sectors – experimented with this approach. Across the ocean in the UK, Tony Buzan developed the concept of mind mapping – a brain-friendly way to digest and structure content.

As the focus was on improving the effectiveness of meetings and processes, many of them created templates, icons and maps to support and structure group dynamics.

In the eighties, the fields of facilitation and consulting bloomed and boomed. Visual facilitation surfed on this wave and by the nineties, visual methodologies had really taken off. Today, graphic recording and facilitation is a valued skill, with many applications across sectors. Professionally, thousands now work as visual practitioners and the number is increasing every day.

I will share a few definitions that are often used in the visual practitioner's playing field.

DIOKIFY

DYNAMIC OF

ONS

FALLING ACTION

DENOU

AMATIC RC

WHAT

PARADISE BY THE DASHBOARD LIGHT

S

SETTING ELEMENTS THEME

CONFLICT
[INTERNAL/EXTERNAL]

SOMEBODY WANTED BUT SO

SPEAK WITH IMPACT

ENTERTAIN ＊ PERSUADE
STORYTELLING WITH HUMOR   KNOWLEDGE & STORYTELLING

NG

USE YOUR FACE

WAKE UP YOUR FACE

Fin

E

your SPACE

GIVE THE CHILD A NAME

If you google the use of drawings at work, these terms might come up:
- Visual harvesting
- Graphic recording
- Visual facilitation
- Sketch noting
- Doodling
- And many more....

These names refer to the methods and roles that you can assume in the process. I have listed the five most common terms:

- **Visual harvesting** is not only the name of our company, it is also used as a broader term for the different methods and roles we play as a visual practitioner.

- **Visual/graphic facilitation:** the person who draws is also a facilitator – the leader of the process of the visual conversation. A visual facilitator is usually most helpful in small groups of people (such as a management team or a strategic team), leading them through a strategic process, and draws the most important insights and decisions throughout their journey. The visual facilitator often takes people through the process using templates or patterns, as well as post-its or flip charts.

- **Visual/graphic recorder:** we also refer to this as "the fly on the wall".

  The person who draws does not lead the process. She brings to life a visual translation of what is being said, what is happening and what is experienced, by means of words and drawings. The drawings are made on a large sheet of paper, a foam board or an iPad so that the participants can follow the visualisation. The term 'scribing' is often used to describe this job.

- **Sketch notes** are comparable to visual reporting but on a smaller scale (like paper, or iPad). The person and the drawings are not visible to the audience. The drawings are then processed in a report, video, or presentation, for example.

- **Doodling** comprises notes, drawings or sketches that people make for themselves, to be able to listen, remember or trigger ideas. Several studies have shown that they are indispensable for retaining information, concentrating and creating new ideas.

My mother listens to difficult stories of important people and turns it, in real time, into a simple drawing.

(my 10-year old daughter explaining to her teacher what I do for a living)

DOODLE LIKE
A PRESIDENT

Sunni Brown, one of the evangelists of visual thinking, sees doodling as a powerful technique. She describes doodling as 'making spontaneous marks to help yourself think'. And doodling certainly has been the cradle of many intellectual and innovative breakthroughs. Research shows that many scientists, innovators – and even presidents – draw during meetings to keep focus or as a catalyst for their thinking process.

Recently, we've seen just how valuable doodling can be. Former US president Barack Obama's quirky pencil sketches on a sheet of White House stationery were sold for USD 11,113.

Did you know?

Before the widespread availability of paper, 12th-century monks in European monasteries used intricate drawings to prepare illustrated, illuminated manuscripts on vellum and parchment. Drawing has also been used extensively in the field of science, as a method of discovery, understanding and explanation.

CREATIVITY IS INTELLIGENCE HAVING FUN.

ALBERT EINSTEIN

THE ART OF ONE-P·A·G·E STRATEGY
HEATHER COLELLA – SANDRA DONATELLI
3
CHOOSE A VIEWPO
AND ANSWER A Q
(OR TWO)
2
CUSTOMER INTIMACY
HOW WE WIN
PRODUCT CHAMPION/LEADER
HOW DO WE INVEST OUR $
LESS TIME NEEDED
EXPLAIN IT
SIMPLIFY THE CORE THINGS
COMMON FOCUS
BE ON 1 PAGE
WHY?
MAKE TECHNOLOGY APPROACHABLE
BRINGING VALUE TO THE RIGHT THINGS
→ COMMUNICATE
BE THE MEMORABLE 15'
BUSINESS STRATEGY
STRATEGIC PLANS
OPERATIONAL PLANS
CREATE A SPACE FOR YOU AT THE EXECUTIVE TABLE
WHY-HOW-WH

A TEACHER'S PURPOSE

A teacher came to see me recently. She told me that it was becoming more and more difficult to hold the attention of her students. She changed her methods regularly and made her lessons as interactive as possible as she had noted that young people wanted novelty. Understandable enough. Technology is advancing at a dizzying speed and young people absorb information in a completely different manner. She wondered whether using drawings might help her to keep her students attentive and interested in the lessons so that they could retain the information better and achieve good results more easily.

She had a clear goal in mind when she began my training. The next day, she gave the lesson in French grammar visually. As soon it was over, the 13-year-old children in the class asked her if they were allowed to take a picture of the whiteboard. They really liked the visual way the content was presented and wanted to have it on their smartphones.

Begin with the end in mind

It's not my purpose to get people drawing just for fun – although it is a lot of fun. My 'reason why' is to challenge the way we currently communicate and collaborate at work. I believe that we have far more potential for effective communication than we are actually achieving. And I hope that by using our visual skills, we will transform meetings so that they become more fun, less boring and more impactful than they often are today.

My challenge to you is this:
1. Before you start, think about your reason why
2. Explore how drawing could help you achieve that
3. Define exactly what you are going to do (draw).

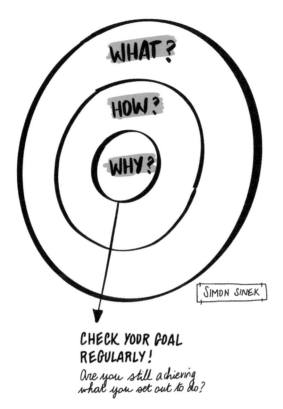

CHECK YOUR GOAL
REGULARLY!
Are you still achieving
what you set out to do?

These three steps are based on the Golden Circle model devised by author and speaker Simon Sinek*. Starting with **why** will clarify **what** you do and **how** you do it.

Why do you do what you do? Why do you jump out of bed in the morning? What do you believe in? Then consider how drawing can help you to realise your why – how it can help you to become even more successful or more impactful in what you do.

*If you are not familiar with Simon Sinek and his work, watch one of his TED talks on www.ted.com. Highly recommended!

Can you earn a living doing this? Is this your job?

Yes, this is my full-time job, and yes, I can earn a living from it. And I am very fortunate and consider myself privileged that my job is what I like to do most.

DO NOT WAIT.
THE TIME WILL NEVER
BE "JUST RIGHT".
START WHERE YOU
STAND, AND WORK WITH
WHATEVER TOOLS YOU
MAY HAVE AT YOUR
COMMAND, AND BETTER
TOOLS WILL BE FOUND
AS YOU GO ALONG.

GEORGE HERBERT (WELSH POET)

WELL, WHAT ARE YOU WAITING FOR?

When I ask people why they want to draw at work, they give more than enough reasons. My flip chart is usually not big enough to note down all the answers. And yet, only a small minority actually does draw. At the beginning of a course, I ask my students what holds them back.
The most frequent answers are:
- It's too time consuming
- Are they going to take me seriously?
- I cannot or do not like to draw
- I can never write nicely
- Is it appropriate in the sector in which I work?
- I do not want to lose eye contact with my audience during consultation
- I do not have the right material
- I do not know where to begin
- I tried it once, but they laughed at me.

Childish?
I once proceeded to draw for employees at a sheltered workplace. One of them shouted, "Do you really think we need drawings to understand you?". They felt that they were being patronised and treated like children. This approach made them feel simple and ignorant. I was told in no uncertain terms that drawing was for toddlers. It was the only time I ever experienced so much resistance.

 • Spell out what you are going to do and explain why.

DO NOT CROSS! • ...OT CROSS!

DO NOT CROSS! • DO NOT CROSS!

WHAT is STOPPING you?

WHO DARES WINS

Some years ago, I was invited to a meeting of the board of directors of a non-profit organisation. Previously, we had gone through the process of how to define values and behaviour with the employees, naturally in a visual manner. The members of the board wanted a progress report, so they asked me to give a presentation during their meeting. This was held in a small room above a bar, late on a Friday afternoon.

When I walked into the small, dark room, I felt the heat and lack of oxygen that are so typical of long meetings, too few breaks and a projector that has been on for hours. The attendees gave little sign that they had any energy left and most of them fidgeted constantly with their smartphone.

I can still see myself walking in with my roll of paper and markers. "Give us your USB stick, ma'am, and we will connect it to our computer and projector," I was told.

"I will not be doing a PowerPoint presentation," I said. "But I do need a blank wall." I looked around the room to see where I could hang up the poster.

I wish I could have drawn the faces of the participants when I began to roll out my 4-metre wide presentation. I witnessed the mood go from scepticism, to interest and on to enthusiasm during the presentation. I even earned a small round of applause when I finished.

I am telling this now as if I did not mind at the time – but nothing could be further from the truth. At the time, holding that roll under my arm in that dark meeting room that was arranged entirely for a PowerPoint presentation, I felt completely out of place. But with a pinch of daring, and belief in what I do, I went ahead. This is but one story. I could tell you many more – and I am convinced that there will be even more to come.

PS There is a nice follow-up to the story. Some months later, I was contacted by one of the members of the Board who worked in another company. He asked me whether I could come along and do "my thing" in his company too...

As the title of this chapter suggests, you need to have guts to use drawings. People do not expect it in a formal business context. Sometimes, they will laugh out loud, because they are not comfortable with it. At such times, you need a good dose of courage. Especially if you are still not completely convinced that you can pull it off...

Keep at it, believe in yourself, and learn from your mistakes. You will be astonished by the impact of your drawings and next time you will be more self-assured when you address the group.

Reason
vision
First steps
START-UPS
JAMES DIMON'S letter
GOOD IS GOOD enough
REACT BEFOR
it's too late!
THE NEW BUSINESS MODEL IS ABOUT COLLECTING DATA
CUSTOMER BECOME MARKETI & SALES
START WITH THE CUSTOMERS FRUSTRATIONS
CUSTOMER
LEVERAGE THE ECOSYS

DO NOT GO TO WAR WITHOUT WEAPONS

Get the right materials to make your skills work. They will make a huge difference.

Think of a tennis player, like Roger Federer. I assume he can play tennis with pretty much any type of racket. But when he really wants to perform at his best, he will surely play with his favourite racket, with specific strings at exactly the right tension. Although I do not want to compare myself with Federer, I find that working with the right tools makes the job easier and drawings look more powerful. Investing in them really pays off.

Did you often draw when you were a child?

Yes, I liked drawing when I was a child. When I was bored, I would draw on any material I could find: beer mats, pieces of cardboard or even of wood, scraps of paper. But I did not develop my drawing skills further. When I was about 15, I stopped drawing. It was only when I was 33 that I got the itch and went back to doing something creative. I went to evening school to study graphic design... and there I often got feedback that my drawing skills could do with some honing.

FOAMCORE

PAPER

CLEANING CLOTH

TAPE

MAKE iT STICK!

MAKE "CORNERS" WITH YOUR TAPE TO FIX PAPER ON THE WALL.

BE SMARTER THAN MURPHY

Even when you have all the skills and materials to put a fine visual report on paper, you still need to take a number of external factors into account. Forewarned (and prepared) is forearmed...

Substantive factors:
Who is the **target group**?

Who am I drawing for? What typifies them? Do they have any preferences in terms of style, colour, and wording?
When I prepare a visual report for a local kindergarten, I make different choices to when I draw for the management team of a major bank.

What is the **house style** of the company you are drawing for? If you provide a report during external meetings (for instance with clients), then make sure you use colours that correspond to the house style of that company. It will be appreciated.

What is the **purpose** of the visual report? Is the report to be used as a memory aid for the people who attended the meeting? Or will it be used for people who were not present at the meeting?
Each situation requires a completely different approach to reporting. Insufficient context (such as catchphrases) may be wrongly interpreted or not understood by people who were not in the room, or do not know the context of that moment.

What is your role? Fringe activities or in the spotlight?

MURPHY'S LAW

- ☑ IF ANYTHING CAN GO WRONG, IT WILL GO WRONG!

- ☑ NOTHING IS AS EASY AS IT LOOKS.

- ☑ EVERYTHING TAKES LONGER THAN YOU EXPECT.

Organisational factors

Companies often do not have a decent flip chart or whiteboard. In such cases, my drawing paper is affixed to the wall with sturdy adhesive tape.

Once I had to draw in a room where the walls were covered with a thick fabric wallpaper. It was impossible to draw on it. "I'll have to do it on the ground," I said to myself. I wound up spending two hours on my knees... Which was annoying and not very elegant. If that were not enough, the markers ran through onto the floor covering.

To prevent such a horror story from recurring, I have drawn up a checklist titled "I'm smarter than Murphy". What can you take into account beforehand?

( ) Light: sufficient to recognise and select the right colours

( ) Sound, acoustics, possible disturbing noise in the room

( ) View of the group

( ) Your view of the screen, the group, the speaker or facilitator

( ) Flip chart, whiteboard, place to affix your paper

( ) Space, location where you will be working

Do you get the presentations in advance to go over them?

Sometimes I receive presentations beforehand. But to be honest, I do not delve extensively into the content. I have noted that the more I know about what is coming, the less well I listen and summarise. In addition, the presentation is seldom representative of what is really being said. What I prefer to know beforehand is who is to speak (with names), for how long (so I know how much space I can use), and what the title and the subject are.

IMPROVISING WITHOUT ANYONE MAKING A PLAN
IT MAKES YOU
HOW CAN IT POSSIBLY SPOIL YOUR LIFE ??!
SOUTH AFRICAN CONNECTION THROUGH Singing
EMPATHY, COMPASSION
ALL SUPPORTING EACH OTHER

SE ROSE ROSE ROSE
HEN SHALL I SEE THEE WED
E, MARRY THAT YOU WILT
WHEN I AM DEAD
SHOW YOUR TRUE
COLOR
SHIFTING
OST VALUABLE
T IN HU
HOW
OTHERW
LEARN
TO TRUST
YOURSELF
DIFFEREN
A BULL
& AN ORC
BECOME SO
UNIQ
& AUTHENTIC

The 10 building blocks of visual communication

Building block 1
LETTERS ARE IMAGES TOO

Before you start drawing, learn to write.

Drawings and text have always gone together. If you do not combine your drawings with text, people will not remember them. The one reinforces the other.

- Write in BLOCK LETTERS, preferably, unless your handwriting is very clear.

- Make sure that you close your letters for the sake of legibility.

- Choose 2 fonts for titles and one for the rest of the text. Make sure you can write rapidly but not at the expense of legibility.

- Be consistent in terms of style and make your letters the same size. Our brain retains patterns. As soon as the pattern is broken, we find it more difficult to recognise words or make links.

- Pay attention to the distance between the letters. They must be neither too close nor too far from each other.

- Lift your pen and write the letters line by line.

Ready to go?

- Choose a marker that fits well in your hand
- Look for letters on packaging, magazines, digital fonts...
- For letters with shadow effects, make sure that the shadow is always on the same side of the letter
- Do you like to write double letters filled with colours? Then write the word first in colour and then go around it with a black marker. That is far easier than the other way around.
- You may vary the setting, distance and size of the letters if you want to stress the meaning of the word.

START TO DRAW

CLOSE YOUR
LETTERS
LETTERS

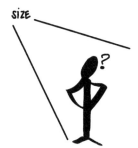

SIZE

?

D I S T A N C E

DISTANCE

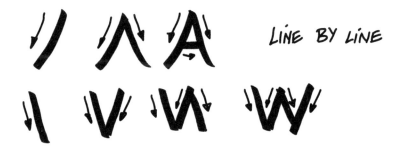

LINE BY LINE

CONSISTENT?

Core ideas
Speed, legibility, consistency

Building block 2
PEOPLE LIKE PEOPLE

People want to see people.
Drawing people attracts their attention and will ensure that your message will remain in their memory for longer.

But how do you draw a figure quickly without making it look like a toddler's attempt? A number of examples are given below that are ever so simple but look very professional. The easiest thing to do is to start with the torso, then the head, and afterwards the arms and legs.

- Use the same figure consistently in a drawing.

- Place people in the room by using a background. Just draw a simple line behind the figure.

- Make sure that the arms start at the shoulders.

- Draw your figure in "small pieces": first the body, then the head, the arms and legs.

- Keep it simple.

Core ideas
Speed, simplicity, consistency

CHOOSE A BODY + ADD A HEAD + DRAW ARMS & LEGS

STEP BY STEP

PICK YOUR STYLE

LET'S MOVE!

Play with emotions

Happiness, sadness, surprise, anger, disgust and fear are the 6 basic emotions. These basic emotions are universal. They are shown and recognised in the same way around the world, irrespective of your cultural background.

We use our mouths and eyebrows in particular to express a certain emotion. The nose is used only to express disgust.

You can increase the emotion (for example, very happy) by enlarging the mouth in the face. If you wish to decrease the emotion, then draw the mouth smaller.

USE THE WHOLE BODY TO INCREASE THE EMOTION

START TO DRAW

YOU CAN FIND INSPIRATION IN EVERYTHING. IF YOU CAN'T, THEN YOU'RE NOT LOOKING PROPERLY.

PAUL SMITH

Do you understand everything you hear and draw?

No, not really. There are times that I still do not really understand half of what I hear. It is not necessary to understand all the details. It all comes down to sketching an overall picture of the story and capturing the gist of it. And usually, you do not find this in the detail, but from a helicopter view.

Building block 3
IF YOU WANT TO BE AN ICON...

Icons are small drawings used to support the text. As mentioned in the section about "letters", text and drawing make a powerful mix. Such icons are intended to give abstract aspects concrete form. Just like letters, they have to be put on paper quickly. So do not get lost in details. Simplicity is an asset.

Clichés are okay for icons. Recognisability is essential. So give your desire to think out of the box a rest and simply draw an image that everyone would come up with.

Suppose that you are looking for an icon for the term "team building". You can approach it from different angles and arrive at different icons. For example:

- What do you hear literally in the word? How would you present that word?
- Which feeling do you associate with the word? Which emotion is linked with it?
- What happens when you work together as a team? What is the result?

Core ideas
Speed, simplicity, cliché is okay

- Draw in full lines. Avoid sketching because it makes your drawing less clear.

- The aim is not to produce something beautiful or perfect. The message is at issue, not the drawing.

- No inspiration? Take a look at Google Images, Pinterest, the noun project...

- Start with simple images to develop your own style: a coffee cup, an ice-cream, an umbrella, a desk lamp... Then move on to people and more abstract concepts.

- "Beware of iconitis": You need not provide a figure or an icon for every word. Strive for a balanced whole of text and drawing.

Icons and context

Icons will look different depending on the context in which they are used. For instance, the word "partnership" will be given a different icon in the business world than in the medical sector.

You must also take the cultural context into account. For instance, once I chose a flying figure for the concept of 'freedom'. The icon was for a Turkish company. A colleague told me that it was not the best choice, because that figure looked like an angel. Drawing angels is sacrilegious in countries like Turkey.

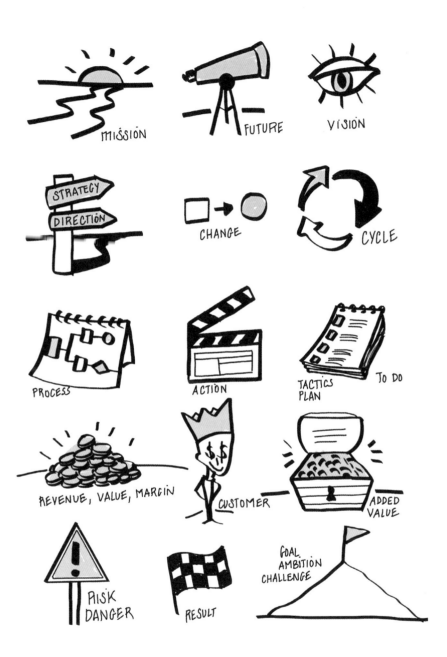

MISSION

FUTURE

VISION

STRATEGY
DIRECTION

CHANGE

CYCLE

PROCESS

ACTION

TACTICS
PLAN

TO DO

REVENUE, VALUE, MARGIN

CUSTOMER

ADDED
VALUE

RISK
DANGER

RESULT

GOAL
AMBITION
CHALLENGE

OPEN · ACCESS

ENERGY

MAIL

MOBILE

DIGITAL

CALCULATE
MONITOR

REFLECT

COMPANY
FACTORY

TIMING
CALENDAR

ROAD MAP
GUIDANCE

DIRECTION

CHOICES

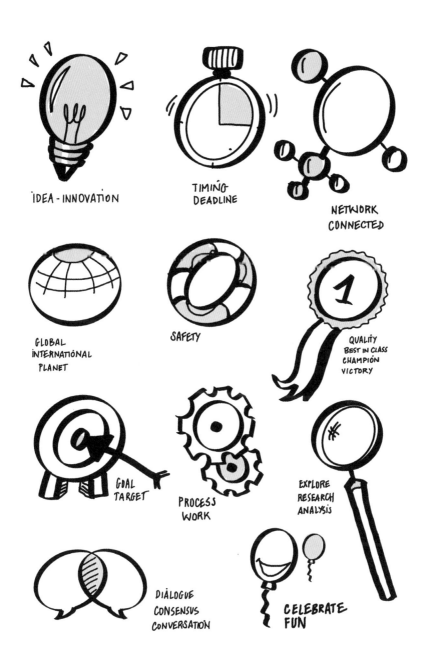

IDEA - INNOVATION

TIMING DEADLINE

NETWORK CONNECTED

GLOBAL INTERNATIONAL PLANET

SAFETY

QUALITY BEST IN CLASS CHAMPION VICTORY

GOAL TARGET

PROCESS WORK

EXPLORE RESEARCH ANALYSIS

DIALOGUE CONSENSUS CONVERSATION

CELEBRATE FUN

ROBOTS

FUTURE

BLOCKCHAIN

NETWORK

CONNECTION

AI

MOBILE

DIGITAL

DISRUPTION

DISRUPTED

DATA

DATA

PRIVACY · SAFETY

CHANGING WORLD

SELF-DRIVING

SHARING ECONOMY

How does your brain work?
What do you do first?
Listen or draw?

—

This is probably the most frequently asked question. For me, it works as follows: I can listen attentively only if I can draw at the same time. The images come to me automatically today. But I have also had to teach myself which drawings go with them. Creativity is like a muscle. The more you use it, the more flexible it becomes. More and more images emerge in my mind from making new associations with words each time. And when I do not know how to draw certain things, the internet is my closest friend.

HELP · CARE

DEAL
AGREEMENT

ADVICE · TIP

CONVERSATION
DIALOGUE

STRENGTH

SHARE KNOWLEDGE

MINDSHIFT

CONNECTION

TEACHER
CONSULTANT

EMPOWERED
LEADER
INITIATIVE

SERVICE

BALANCED

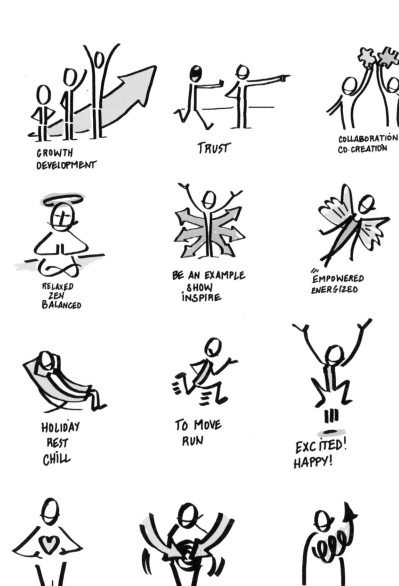

GROWTH
DEVELOPMENT

TRUST

COLLABORATION
CO-CREATION

RELAXED
ZEN
BALANCED

BE AN EXAMPLE
SHOW
INSPIRE

EMPOWERED
ENERGIZED

HOLIDAY
REST
CHILL

TO MOVE
RUN

EXCITED!
HAPPY!

PASSION
TALENT

INTUITION

FLOW

Building block 4
ANTHROPOMORPHISM

Anthro... what?

The definition in Wikipedia runs as follows:

Anthropomorphism is the attribution of human traits, emotions or intentions to non-human entities. It is considered to be an innate tendency of human psychology.

Anthropomorphism helps us to better understand the world we live in, to categorise and define it in a more human and understandable way.

A lot of big brands use anthropomorphism to make their brand more "friendly", "human", "happy". Applying this technique, you can very easily draw the status of an object, an organisation, a system, like a dynamic company, a stressed world...

ANTHRO...

Building block 5
FRAME IT

Frames provide an extra dimension. They complete your drawing and confer an overall professional structure.

When you wish to highlight a figure or icon, make the frame around it as small as possible. It may sound illogical, but the smaller you draw the frame around an icon, the greater the focus on the icon or figure itself.

Here once again, consistency is the golden rule. Different frames may bring a different weight to bear on the things they contain.

Text balloons and banners are also frames. So opt for consistency here too.

- Draw your frames only at the very end. You never know what the most important items in your visual report will be.

- First the text, then the frame.

- Not everything has to be framed. A frame gives the impression that things belong together, which is not always the case.

CLOSED   OPEN

An open frame gives another
dimension to your drawing,
compared to a closed frame.

A FRAME FILLED WITH COLOUR HIGHLIGHTS YOUR OBJECT EVEN MORE!

Building block 6

SAY GOODBYE TO BORING LISTS

Lists need not always be linear.

A linear list immediately gives the impression of hierarchy or sequence.

If this is not relevant, you can opt just as well for summaries which are not neatly arranged underneath each other.

The opposite is also true. If you draw up a Top 10 list, it makes sense to arrange the items underneath each other.

You can use strong bullet points, frames, and so on to make a simple yet visually attractive list.

- Make sure that things that belong together are depicted in the same way. Consistency is important here once again.

- If you are working with a target group that is very attached to structure and order, it is sometimes better to work with a linear list. People with autism, for instance, will retain an overview better when the items of the list are placed neatly underneath each other.

This is n~~o~~t a list.

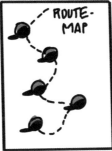

Building block 7
COLOUR FOR MAXIMUM IMPACT

Structure
Colour brings your drawing to life and gives structure. First determine where the focal point should be and use a specific colour to that end. Too much colour gets in the way of structure because the eye roams in every direction.

Mood
Purple, blue, silver and green are cold colours.
Orange, red, gold and yellow are warm colours.

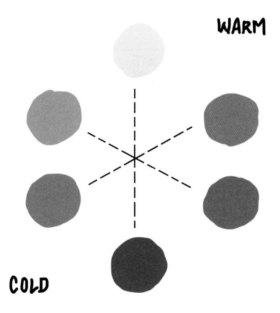

WARM

COLD

START TO DRAW

If you use only warm colours, your drawing will come across as garish. If you use only cold colours, your drawing will feel muted. So try to strike a balance between the two by accentuating certain aspects. By and large, warm colours attract the most attention. Use this option to highlight certain works or items.

For a stronger and leaner effect, it is best to opt for black when drawing up the outline of the image and to use colour for the inside.

Associations

Colours have an emotional connotation.

Consider the combination of yellow and blue, for instance. Many people associate this combination with IKEA. Depending on your message, consider that the association with this brand could work against you or help you to make your point.

Suppose that you have to produce a visual report for the supporters of a certain football club, political party or trade union. Here, once again, I opt very consciously not to use certain colours (those of an opponent or competitor). I always take a company's house style into account. My wardrobe permitting, I attune the colour of my outfit to the client I am visiting.

The slogan in the media – and in fashion – is "green costs a pretty penny". A cover where green dominates doesn't seem to attract the eye. Magazines with a green cover therefore sell less quickly. So if you really want to get attention, green is probably not your best choice.

TiP

- Yellow, orange, and green are less suitable for writing except as a filling for titles (outlined with black).

- If the drawing is done very rapidly and simultaneously (at a meeting, for instance), you should limit the number of colours. It will take you a few seconds each time you change colour (and therefore marker) – seconds you need in order to be able to follow the content of the meeting or training.

- Add the colours once the drawing is completed.

- The Neuland brand sells black outliner markers. You can then go over them with a colour without causing stains.

Core ideas
be consistent, choose consciously, do not exaggerate

DRAWING IS RATHER LIKE PLAYING CHESS: YOUR MIND RACES AHEAD OF THE MOVES THAT YOU EVENTUALLY MAKE.

DAVID HOCKNEY

Is this a gift you were born with?

No, I do not think so. I am convinced that many people can learn this. It is true that you have to combine many different skills, in order to be a graphic recorder, for instance. The more of these skills you have in your arsenal, the easier it will be to learn this job.

Building block 8
BRING DIMENSION
WITH SHADOW

Shadows give depth to your drawings and make them look more professional.

There is a golden rule for shadow and accents: always have any light fall on the same side. In other words, if your light source is on the left, draw your shadow on the right side and vice versa.

START TO DRAW

Building block 9

CONNECT WITH
THE FLOW

The flow is "the guiding principle" of your report. You can bring flow
with arrows, dotted lines, numbers, and colours.
In this way, you guide the eye of the viewer and give structure to
your drawing.
It helps the reader of the report to understand where the visual
story begins and where it ends.

- Try to stick to the natural reading direction (left
  to right).

- Only connect different ideas of words when it
  matters. When drawing a panel debate, for instance,
  it is not necessarily relevant to draw lines or arrows in
  between the different opinions.

lonely

START TO DRAW

Building block 10
EMBRACE BLANK SPACE

Blank space may well be my biggest challenge. And it is no easy balance to strike.
Too much blank space will make your drawing look empty and unfinished... as if something is missing.
If there is no blank space, you will lose sight of the forest for the trees and your message will get lost.

It all comes down to providing blank space and sufficient fill-in.

It can help to provide some areas on your sheet that are deliberately kept clear.
Or provide blank space, a no-go zone around the different drawings, icons and words, in which you do not write or draw anything.

Sometimes, blank space is another way to draw attention to something. Such blank space then serves as the frame.

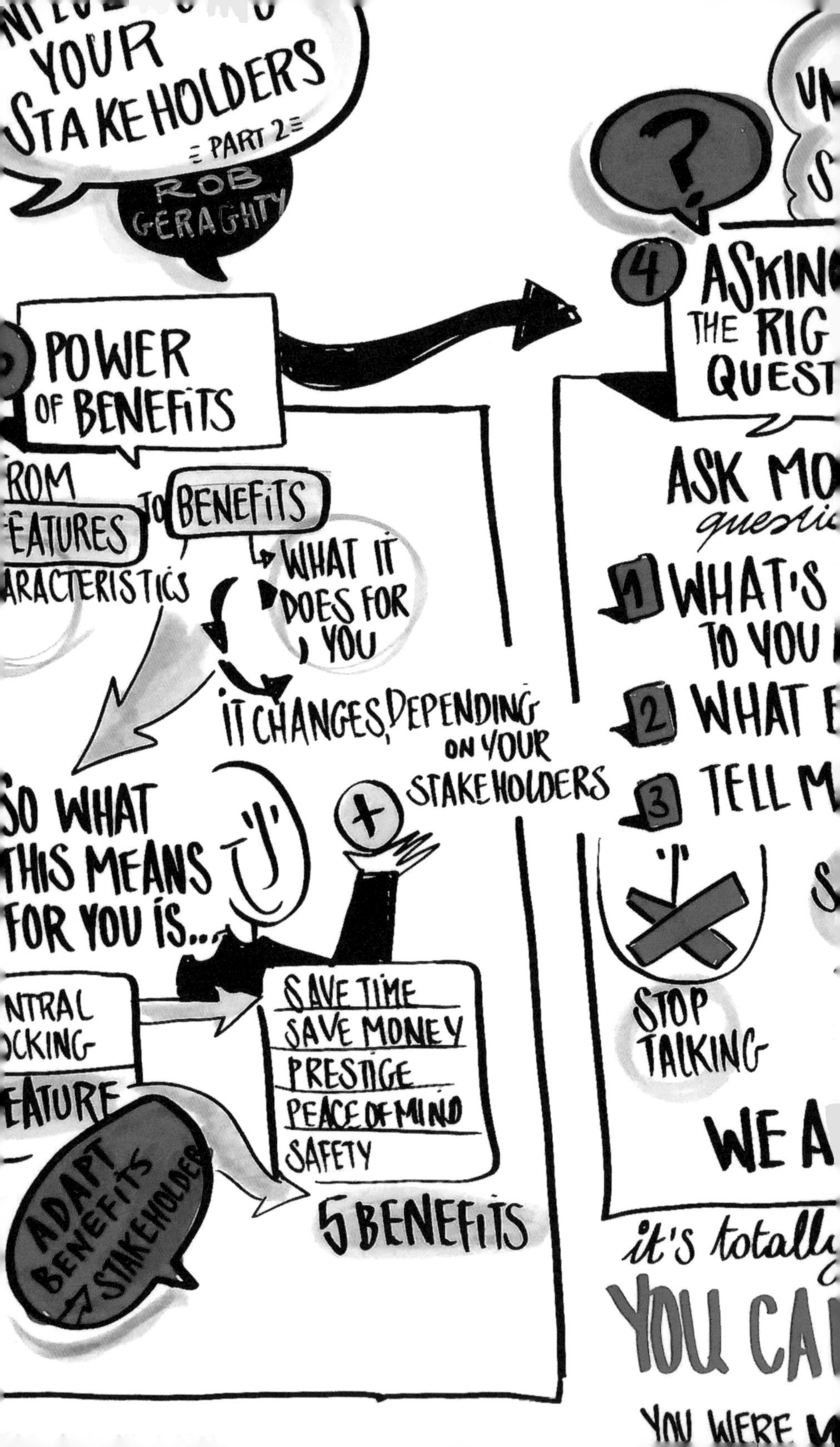
YOUR
STAKEHOLDERS
PART 2
ROB GERAGHTY
POWER OF BENEFITS
ROM
EATURES
TO
BENEFITS
ARACTERISTICS
WHAT IT DOES FOR YOU
IT CHANGES, DEPENDING ON YOUR STAKEHOLDERS
SO WHAT THIS MEANS FOR YOU IS...
NTRAL
OCKING
EATURE
SAVE TIME
SAVE MONEY
PRESTIGE
PEACE OF MIND
SAFETY
5 BENEFITS
ADAPT BENEFITS STAKEHOLDER
4
ASKING
THE RIG
QUEST
ASK MO
questio
1 WHAT'S
TO YOU
2 WHAT
3 TELL M
STOP TALKING
WE A
it's totally
YOU CA
YOU WERE M

STAND
HOLDER

⑤ BOOST *your* BODYLANGUAGE

MAKE YOURSELF BIGGER

SKILLS

EY
CON

ORTAN
UT...

M
CO
a

ORE ABOUT

ARIZE
CK

GET DATA

⑥ INCREASE YOUR AUTHORITY

EXPERTISE

BORROW AUTHORITY

"GA
↳

ALL IN SALES

your control!

O THIS !

TO BE THE

BE SPECIFIC
• 67%. ... TOLD US.
• 3 ACTIONS WER

YOU DON'T NEED TO (ONLY) BE ABLE TO DRAW

If you can make simple, clear drawings with a certain ease, you have a sizeable advantage when you decide to start with visual reporting. But it is not the only – nor the most important – skill. You will need to develop a number of other skills.

Listening: I am a social nurse by training, and I worked as a social worker at the Public Welfare Agency in the first 5 years of my career. I listened to the stories of my clients each and every day, and then translated them into reports intended to ensure that they got the right help and support. I am firmly convinced that I laid sound foundations during that time for the work that I do today. Listening is one of the most important skills if you want to make visual reports on a discussion or a meeting.

Summarising: Determine what you want to give back to your audience. Not all information is relevant during a lengthy meeting. It would be an impossible task, for that matter, to recount every word and every detail of the discussion. And you will fail to achieve your objective. You have to look for the core ideas and reproduce them.

Structuring: As in a written report, a visual report has to have a clear structure. In a text, such a structure is obtained by means of titles, paragraphs and spacing. In a visual report, you bring structure and hierarchy by a balanced and well thought out use of colour, typeface and frames.

Writing nicely and rapidly: Sometimes, you have to proceed really rapidly and then you have no time to add drawings to your report. Your ability to put a balanced and well-groomed typeface on paper will save the day. Beautiful handwriting is a drawing in itself when you highlight it with a frame or a banner and add a bit of colour.

It is not possible to master all these skills at the same time. You can compare the process with learning a foreign language: in the beginning you need a certain vocabulary and have to get the hang of the basics. The more you practise, the richer your vocabulary will get. At the outset, you will not conjugate your verbs yet, and your sentence structure will not tally exactly but you will gradually notice that you are becoming more proficient. After some time, it will be nearly second nature to you. The mantra is: "practice makes progress."

Are you an artist by training?

No, I am a nurse and social worker by training, and that's where I get my listening skills from.

EVERY CHILD IS AN ARTIST. THE PROBLEM IS TO REMAIN AN ARTIST ONCE HE GROWS UP.

PABLO PICASSO

AND NOW DOWN TO BUSINESS!

Challenging meeting? Draw!

You have to face numerous challenges when you hold meetings, give presentations, coach teams, and so on. We list some of these challenges in order to suggest possible visual solutions.
The list is limited, so there are many more possibilities. Proceed creatively with possible combinations to find out what works for you.

Ask yourself each time: what can I prepare (before the meeting); what do I do (during the meeting); and what can I still do (after the meeting)?

(New) participants have to be briefed about a project
Graphical timeline

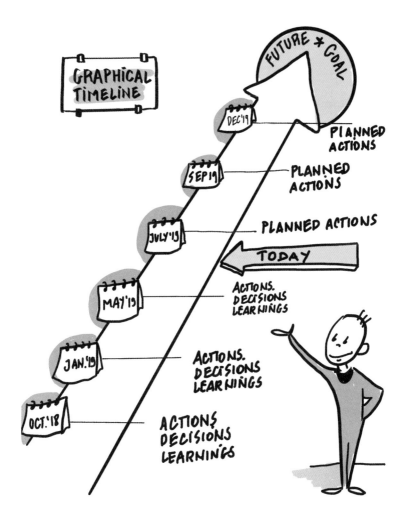

Keep the focus on the meeting process

Parking area (where ideas that are not on the agenda are placed)

START TO DRAW

Establish a basic meeting culture
Visualise the objectives, agenda, rules and roles of the meeting

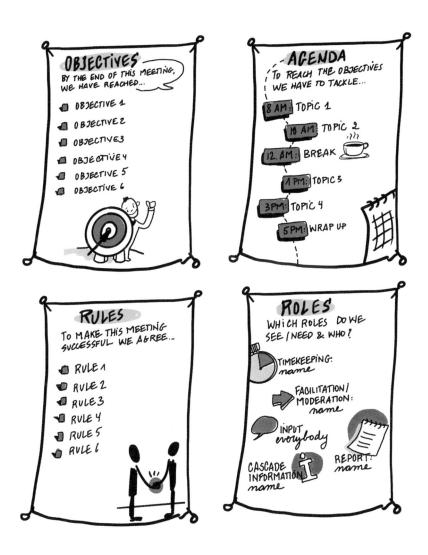

Free people from the operational problems and functioning
Vision mandala

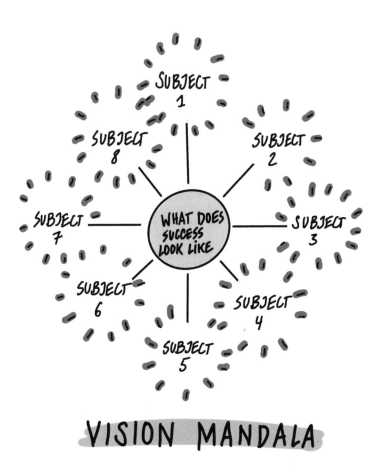

VISION MANDALA

Coordinate a project with different stakeholders
Visual agenda, schedule, framework

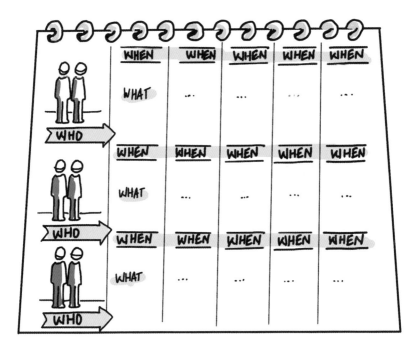

VISUAL AGENDA
with
DIFFERENT STAKEHOLDERS

Create ownership and drive action
Graphical action plan

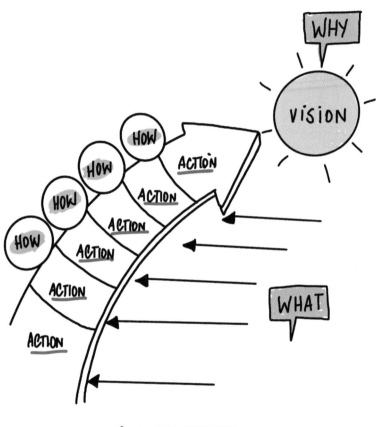

Set priorities and preferences in a multitude of ideas
Grid with energy and affinity (high/low)

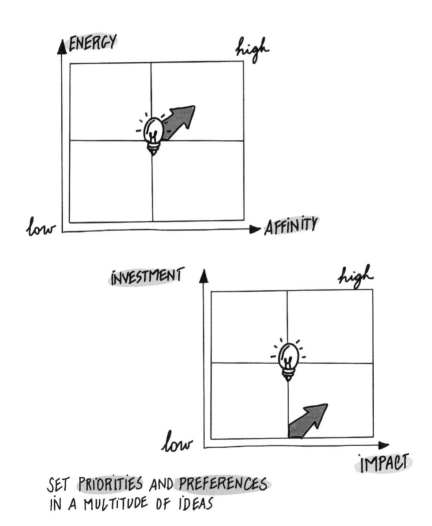

SET PRIORITIES AND PREFERENCES
IN A MULTITUDE OF IDEAS

You want an open, honest discussion on a topic, which you can revisit
Visual report of the conversation

START TO DRAW

Visualise opinions or expectations
Bring opinions to the table

DRAWING IS LIKE BOILING DOWN: ONLY THE ESSENCE REMAINS.

LILY MARTENS

How can you be so fast and still capture the essence of an idea?

Speed has to do with skill, on the one hand, but even more so with choices: what do I draw, what not? What do I summarise, what do I forego, and which details are perhaps important after all? To be complete, you must therefore summarise well and, above all, correctly. I often ask clients: what unique message must everyone who looks at the drawing retain?
That is the question you should ask yourself when you give your message visual form: what is the one thing that I want the viewer to remember?

TRANSFORMING LI
HIL ANSEN PART 2
1 DRAW YOUR PET
2. WRITE SOMETHING YOU WANT TO ACHIEVE NEXT YEAR
3 TURN THE PENCIL ON IT'S SIDE SCRIBBLE OVER THE MEDIUM DARK
4. DRAW YOURSELF
5 SHADE OVER IT MEDIUM DARK
6 DRAW WHERE YOU GREWUP
&SCRIBBLE IT OVER
7 draw SOMETHING YOU CAN'T LIVE WITHOUT
&.FILL IN
let
CR
AR
9 WRITE
8 THINK OF SOMEON
YOU'RE EL
TO & THIN
FILL IN OUTSIDE AS DARK AS YOU C

ATIONS into OPPORTUNITIES
MAKE THE
ACTION
to RESHAPE
CULTURE
NAME
10 DRAW THE PERSON NEXT TO YOU
11 TAKE A PICTURE OF YOUR PIECES

TRAINING PLAN: GET GOING!

During my training sessions, people often tell me: "Thanks for your tips, Axelle. But what now? How do I get going?"

Everyone has a different way of learning, of course, but in essence the process boils down to: practice and repeat!

To make it easier for you, I have opted to arrange everything in manage-able segments and to craft a training scheme that ranges from easy to (more) difficult.

DAY 1
Letters

DAY 2
Banners, frames and text balloons

It is easy to start with letters. As I have already pointed out, it suffices to choose three font types that you feel at ease with. You can still adapt and spruce them up by adding lines, shadows, or dots. You can choose to write down the entire alphabet first, and then practise with the letters by writing a couple of nice quotes. You will see better how the different letters interrelate and you can also practise with distances between letters and words.

Now you can put your quotes in a frame, a banner or a text balloon. Do not limit yourself to round or rectangular text balloons or frames. A text in a heart or a cloud immediately acquires an extra dimension. A number of examples of frames I often use are provided. You can also use shadow and colour.

DAY 3 AND 4
People and emotions

In the chapter on people, I pointed out that you can draw figures in all sorts of simple ways that look very professional nonetheless. Choose one you feel most comfortable with and draw him in different positions (standing, sitting, thinking, jumping, dancing, running, cycling, falling). The internet and especially Google Images are good sources of inspiration. Once you get the hang of it, it will become second nature to you.

Now you can add an emotion to your figures. Practise with the basic emotions first, because these are the ones you will use most often.

DAY 5 AND 6
Icons

First copy icons of everyday things from the internet or from my examples. Choose 25 icons and practise with them until you hardly have to think about them any more. The key words are speed and simplicity. So do not draw too many details. Each time you have drawn 5 icons, repeat the 5 previous ones. In this way, you will have an arsenal of icons by the end of day 5 – ready to be deployed by your pen.

You will proceed in the same way during day 6, but for more abstract notions such as passion, hope, motivation, leadership, and flexibility. You can draw up a word list first or you can try to draw what you pick up at random. You'll already have come a long way with the icons that I provided and those you can find on the internet.

DAY 7 AND 8
Mix and match

DAY 9 AND 10
The total picture

And now for tougher work! You will listen to spoken texts as much as possible today. These can be debates, keynotes (for example, www.ted.com), meetings – even songs. Listen carefully to the text to grasp the essence. You can use two typefaces: one for the core ideas and the other to render details. At the end, you will structure the text by adding frames, banners and a flow. Now finish your visual report with colour and shadow.

You will now repeat the exercise of the last week and add icons and figures to your drawing. I often advise people to draw a title and a figure before starting, so they do not have to begin by staring at a blank sheet of paper. Try to strike a balance between text and drawing. It is best to work with only two colours at the outset. You can always add extra colours (and shadow) afterwards.

The time limit of 10 days is only a guideline. You can decide for yourself how much time you wish to spend on the process.

Good luck!

-GNITION BOOTC

Day 1

ETER HINSSEN

I'm a **NERD!**
AND ONLY HAD A BOSS AND A NORMAL JOB FOR 48 MONTHS

I'M FASCINATED BY PROGRESS

and **ACT**

HOW CAN YOU ACCELE ?

ARE YOU CAPABLE TO SEE MORE THAN OTHER PEOPLE CAN SEE?

THE FUTURE always COMES

BOOK ANGED Y LIFE ING DIGITA

QUIT JOB

STARTED A COMPANY & **SOLD** IT TO ALCATEL "WORST DECISION OF MY LIFE"

INVOICE to McKINSEY ☑ !

3rd START-UP 2006-2010

2nd START-UP FAILED 1€

YES BU

MP
DO THEY UNDERSTAND THE POTENTIAL OF NEW THINGS ?
HOW DO THEY KILL START-UP
HY THEY CAN'T DO IT ON THEIR WN?
FAIL
SELF DRIVI TRUC
DRIVI SELF-DR CAR
CH EVOLUTION RE just e beginning
YES ... BUT
MOST VALUABLE BRANDS TOP 6 ⇨ 5 ARE TECH
IGGEST CHALLENGE OF COMPANIES S TO KILL "YES, BUT"
YOUR POINT OF VIEW
ERATE

HAVE NO FEAR OF PERFECTION. YOU WILL NEVER REACH IT.

SALVADOR DALI

PERFECTION
IS DULL

Years ago, I threw a party for the opening of a new office.
I had asked an artist friend of mine if I could hang her work for the occasion.
On the day of the opening, I was turbo charged, trying to arrange everything down to the minutest details.
Everything had to be perfect: the furniture, the paintings, the catering, the tents...
I forgot to enjoy myself, and was left only with stress.

My friend the artist took me aside and said, "Axelle, stop it! Perfection is dull! Don't bother!"

She was right... In striving to make sure everything was perfect, I lost sight of the essence – to enjoy a festive event, speak to my guests and make plans for the future.

The same applies to drawing. We can strive to put a perfect drawing on paper, down to the minutest details... But that is not the essence.
Worse still, it stifles creativity.
The purpose of the drawing is to get a message across. If that message is clear, your drawing is good enough.

So overcome your compulsion for perfection and dare to make mistakes.

How can you learn something like this?

—

You can take courses all over the world, and probably online as well. Start with a book (such as this one) or tutorials but, above all, do a lot of exercises... practise, and practise some more. Each time you draw something, you will make mistakes or run into some obstacle. And that is fantastic, because that is when you learn the most.

FAILING
GRACEFULLY

It hurts when you fail. Just imagine if, as children, we did not get back on the bike after a painful tumble... Nobody in the world would be riding a bike.

Why are we so afraid of getting things wrong?
Because you can be sure of one thing: you are going to fail. And that's just as well. Because the best insights and learning moments occur during and after failure.

The same applies to your visual work. Every time, you will do things that you would have preferred to look different – draw horses that look like dogs, make writing errors.

What it comes down to at such times is a matter of failing gracefully... and, if possible, learning for the next time.

• Provide white labels of different sizes. They help you improve your mistakes: small labels for writing errors, large labels to do full drawings all over again.

• Draw a black area over the mistake and write in white acrylic marker in that black area.

• Get help. If you are not sure that you have written something correctly (for example, in the case of jargon, foreign languages, unknown names, etcetera), ask someone from the public to help you. The same applies when it comes to customs, traditions, internal arrangements or culture that you might not be completely familiar with.

Some years ago, I was drawing at a conference in Abu Dhabi. The topic of the event was sustainability. The question was: how can young people in Abu Dhabi build a greener future for the United Arab Emirates?

The group we were working with consisted of 30 university students: 27 girls and 3 boys. I was told that university students in Abu Dhabi were mainly female because men opted for more technical occupations.
One of the lectures was given by an industrialist. He explained how industry can have a positive impact on ecology, for instance, by innovating in cooperation with the university.
They asked me to make a large drawing that visualised the cooperation between industrialists and students. "Cooperation" is often drawn by showing people shaking hands. I looked around and saw all those female students, so I drew a female student who shook hands with an industrialist...

While I was giving shape to my metre-high drawing with a flowing movement, I felt the energy in the room change – murmuring, giggling, and one student stood up and came to me and said: "sorry, Axelle, we cannot shake hands with a man, so this drawing will not do."

For the sake of clarity: the drawing was about 1m^2, so it could not be solved with a label. And it was silly, because I was well aware that this was not allowed, but in the flow of the drawing, I had completely forgotten about it.
I apologised, and then set out to correct my mistakes. I transformed the female student I had drawn into a male version. Fortunately, men there also wear a long, white robe with a keffiyeh (headscarf) that has red and white squares. I gave the face of the student a moustache, drew checks on the headscarf with a black ribbon around it, ... And the mistake was corrected.

BIBLIOGRAPHY

Brandy Agerbeck, **The Graphic Facilitator's Guide: How to Use Your Listening, Thinking and Drawing Skills to Make Meaning,** Loosetooth.com Library, 2012

Dan Roam, **The Back of the Napkin,** Portfolio, 2009

David Sibbet, **Visual Leaders, New Tools for Visioning, Management and Organization Change,** Wiley, 2013

David Sibbet, **Visual Teams: Graphic Tools for Commitment, Innovation and High Performance,** Wiley, 2011

Bernard Labelle and Guillaume Lagane, **Dites-le en images,** Eyrolles, 2013

MY SOURCES OF INSPIRATION

Since the day I started as a visual practitioner, I have been inspired by several colleagues, artists, all kind of professionals. It would be impossible to name them all. However, I will mention some of them because I'm sure that they could inspire you too...

First of all, my colleagues in the Visual Harvesting team – Martine Van Remoortele, Kristof Braekeleire, Iris Maertens

My colleagues - visual practitioners around the world:
Anthony Weeks
Avril Orloff
Brandy Agerbeck
David Sibbet
Heather Martinez
Kelvy Bird
Nevada Lane
Sam Bradd
Sunni Brown
Tim Hamons
And many, many more

Join the Graphic facilitation group on Facebook and get inspired by thousands of visual practitioners.

Looking for icons/images?
The noun project
Google images
Pinterest 'stickfigures'
Pinterest 'how to draw...'
Wordasimage

THANKS!

With special thanks to ...

Martine Van Remoortele for igniting that creative sparkle inside me 10 years ago, when I first saw a graphic recorder, and for being such a supportive colleague and source of inspiration and honest feedback.

Caroline Storme for your help in writing out the main ideas, key insights and content with your starter's and outsider's view.

Joel, Laura and Cézanne, My husband and two daughters, for their support during the years of searching, developing, working, being absent and being able to follow my passion.

Lily Martens who, a few years ago, helped me to shape the idea of a book and kept on encouraging me to continue... She's also one of the few people who asked me challenging questions when looking at my drawings, which helped me to grow. My favourite question is, "where do you want my eyes to go to?".

Annelies Dollekamp who designed the book and brought it to life... and stayed enthusiastic even after a writer's block of 12 months.

All my clients and partners who worked with me over the past 10 years and believed in the power of visual communication. With special thanks to my colleagues at nexxworks.com who engaged me for so many hours, which I gratefully used to practise, practise, practise... (and where a lot of the live drawings in this book were made.)

THE NEXT 20 PAGES
OF THIS BOOK
ARE ALL YOURS!

Fill them with your favorite
- ◯ letters
- ◯ figures
- ◯ icons
- ◯ frames

and much more.

Have fun. Fail, learn, and enjoy!

D/2019/45/527 – ISBN 978 94 014 6524 3 – NUR 800

Cover and interior design: Annelies Dollekamp - www. zilverstermedia.nl

© Axelle Vanquaillie & Lannoo Publishers nv, Tielt, 2019.

LannooCampus Publishers is a subsidiary of Lannoo Publishers,
the book and multimedia division of Lannoo Publishers nv.

LannooCampus Publishers
Vaartkom 41 box 01.02   P.O. Box 23202
3000 Leuven   1100 DS Amsterdam Belgium
www.lannoocampus.be   Netherlands
www.lannoocampus.com   www.lannoocampus.nl